F/A-18E/F Super Hornet & EA-18G Growler

The US Navy's Primary Fighter/Attack Aircraft

KEN NEUBECK

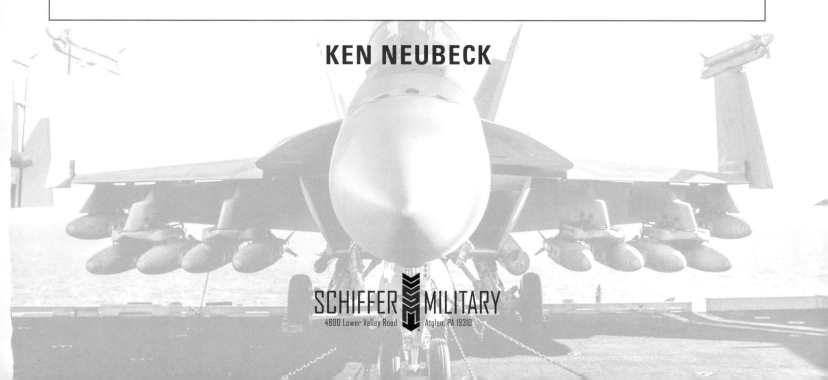

SCHIFFER MILITARY

4880 Lower Valley Road   Atglen, PA 19310

Designed by Justin Watkinson
Type set in Impact/Minion Pro/Univers LT Std
Rear cover image courtesy of Jamie Hunter

ISBN: 978-0-7643-5923-1
Printed in China

Published by Schiffer Publishing, Ltd.
4880 Lower Valley Road
Atglen, PA 19310
Phone: (610) 593-1777; Fax: (610) 593-2002
E-mail: Info@schifferbooks.com
www.schifferbooks.com

For our complete selection of fine books on this and related subjects, please visit our website at www.schifferbooks.com. You may also write for a free catalog.

Schiffer Publishing's titles are available at special discounts for bulk purchases for sales promotions or premiums. Special editions, including personalized covers, corporate imprints, and excerpts, can be created in large quantities for special needs. For more information, contact the publisher.

We are always looking for people to write books on new and related subjects. If you have an idea for a book, please contact us at proposals@schifferbooks.com.

Acknowledgments

The author thanks those individuals who contributed to the book, including John Gourley, Jamie Hunter, as well as the Boeing Company, General Dynamics, and US Navy for the use of photos.

Contents

Introduction

The Super Hornet is an evolutionary redesign of the McDonnell Douglas F/A-18 Hornet, the first production aircraft of which flew in 1980. The original F/A-18 Hornet met the requirement for a multirole fighter to complement the larger and more expensive Grumman F-14 Tomcat, serving in fleet defense interceptor and air superiority roles. The Hornet proved to be effective, but it was it limited in combat radius due to fuel capacity.

The concept of an enlarged Hornet was first proposed in the 1980s, which was marketed by McDonnell Douglas as "Hornet 2000." The Hornet 2000 concept was an advanced F/A-18 with a larger wing and a longer fuselage to carry more fuel and more-powerful engines. This concept meant that it could take over more of the F-14 role.

In addition, the end of the Cold War brought along military budget cuts, and the US Navy faced a number of problems, such as the McDonnell Douglas A-12 Avenger II being canceled in 1991. This aircraft was intended to replace the Grumman A-6 Intruder and Ling-Temco-Vought (LTV) A-7 Corsair II. At this point, the Navy considered updating an existing design as a more attractive approach than a brand-new program. Thus, the F/A-18E/F Super Hornet was proposed as the A-6 replacement, and it was an improvement of the successful previous F/A-18 models.

At the time, the Grumman F-14 Tomcat was the Navy's primary air superiority fighter and fleet defense interceptor, but it was considered older technology, and production was ended in 1991 in favor of producing the F/A-18E/F Super Hornet. The decision to replace the Tomcat with an all-Hornet carrier air wing was controversial, but the move to the Super Hornet was deemed to be cost effective, particularly in the area of maintenance, where fewer man-hours were required. The empty weight of the F-14 was 43,735 pounds, whereas the F-18 Super Hornet is 32,081 pounds.

The legacy F/A-18 Hornet did not have the desired range and often had to carry external fuel tanks to add to the range. Thus, the larger Super Hornet had more room internally for fuel, as well as having two extra wing pylons to carry more ordnance.

Additionally, the Super Hornet, with some simple modification, could be made into a tanker aircraft, in the vein of the A-6D, which had served in the role of the tanker aircraft on indigenous aircraft carriers. Additionally, the Super Hornet aircraft led into the EA-18G Growler, which took over the electronic countermeasures (ECM) role of the EA-6B Prowler. Hence, the basic airframe of the Super Hornet led to models and modifications for several carrier roles.

By 2005, estimates for maintaining the older F-14 Tomcats were running in the range of fifty maintenance man-hours per flight hour, whereas the F/A-18 Super Hornet was in the range of fifteen maintenance man-hours per flight hour. It was harder to retrofit a "glass" cockpit concept into the F-14D version compared to starting off with this type of cockpit in the new F/A-18 Super Hornet. The F-14 was a Cold War–designed aircraft, and the F/A-18E/F employed newer techniques such as composites to make the aircraft lighter.

The Super Hornet was first ordered by the US Navy in 1992, with the F/A-18E being the single-seat version and the F/A-18F being the two-seat version. Even though the Navy retained the F/A-18 designation to help sell the program to Congress as a low-risk "derivative," the truth is that the Super Hornet is essentially a new aircraft. The thinking was that a new designation would have met much resistance in securing funding for a new program, compared to this approach.

CHAPTER 1
Super Hornet Development

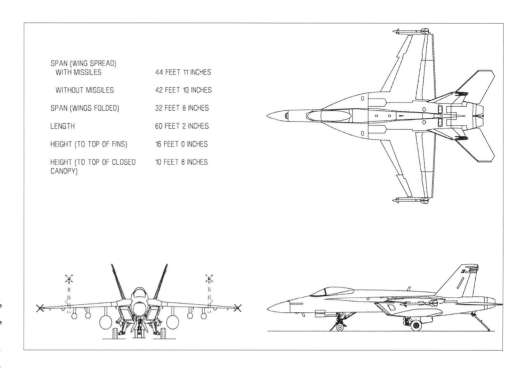

SPAN (WING SPREAD) WITH MISSILES	44 FEET 11 INCHES
WITHOUT MISSILES	42 FEET 10 INCHES
SPAN (WINGS FOLDED)	32 FEET 8 INCHES
LENGTH	60 FEET 2 INCHES
HEIGHT (TO TOP OF FINS)	16 FEET 0 INCHES
HEIGHT (TO TOP OF CLOSED CANOPY)	10 FEET 8 INCHES

The Hornet and Super Hornet share much of the same equipment, such as landing gear, structure, flight instruments, some avionics, ejection seats, radar, and armament. The airframe would be expanded in the Super Hornet, with an empty weight slightly greater than the F-15C.

The F/A-18E Super Hornet first flew on November 29, 1995. Flight testing started in 1996, with the F/A-18E's first carrier landing in 1997. Low-rate production began in March 1997, with full production beginning in September 1997. Testing continued through 1999, finishing with sea trials and aerial-refueling demonstrations. Testing involved 3,100 test flights covering 4,600 flight hours.

The Super Hornet would be operational in force by the turn of the new century, with significant participation in combat action in Afghanistan and the Middle East. There would be foreign sales for this aircraft with Australia, as well as a derivative ECM version to replace the EA-6B.

F/A-18E Specifications

Empty weight	32,081 lbs.
Maximum takeoff weight	66,000 lbs.
Power plant	Two F414-GE-400
Maximum speed	Mach 1.8
Service ceiling	50,000 feet
Range (combat)	1,275 miles

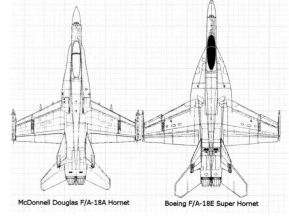

	F/A-18A	F/A-18E
Length	56 feet	60.3 feet
Width	40.4 feet	44.7 feet
Height	15.3 feet	16 feet
Weight (empty)	23,000 lbs.	32,081 lbs.

McDonnell Douglas F/A-18A Hornet   Boeing F/A-18E Super Hornet

Shown here is an F/A-18A Hornet from the Marine Corps squadron VMFA-232 "Red Devils." The F/A-18A began operational service in 1983. Distinguishing features include the circular engine inlets.
US Navy photo by MCS 3rd Class Gretchen M. Roth

The Super Hornet first flew in 1995 and was introduced into the fleet in 1997 as an evolutionary design improvement from the legacy Hornet. While it has many similarities to the legacy aircraft, it is essentially a different aircraft, with more weight and thrust as well as other upgrades. The aircraft has larger rectangular engine inlets, along with an extended leading edge from the forward fuselage. *Ken Neubeck*

Differences between the Hornet and Super Hornet models can be highlighted in side-by-side comparisons. In this head-on view of the F/A-18C Hornet aircraft, the circular engine inlets can be seen, along with the small forward fuselage leading edge on both sides of the fuselage. *John Gourley*

In a similar head-on view of the F/A-18E Super Hornet aircraft, the engine inlets are now rectangular and larger. Additionally, the forward fuselage leading edge is wider on both sides of the fuselage. The wingspan has been increased an additional 4 feet from 40.4 feet to 44.7 feet. *John Gourley*

Boeing company worker is performing checks in the canopy of an F/A-18F Super Hornet in the company factory in St. Louis, Missouri. *Boeing*

Boeing company worker installs panel in the lower fuselage on a Super Hornet in the company production line. *Boeing*

Flight line personnel are working with Boeing company test pilots during fit check of the cockpit in F/A-18F aircraft in final assembly. The company will flight test the aircraft prior to formal delivery to the US Navy. *Boeing*

F/A-18E One-Seat Super Hornet Program History

Type	Quantity	BuNo
EMD	2	165164–165165
EMD	3	163167–165169
USN Production	8	165533–165540
USN Production	8	165652–165659
USN Production	14	165779–165792
USN Production	15	165860–165874
USN Production	14	165896–165909
USN Production	25	165910–165934
USN Production	29	166420–166448
USN Production	12	166598–166609
USN Production	15	166643–166657
USN Production	15	166775–166789
USN Production	25	166817–166841
USN Production	14	166859–166872
USN Production	8	166901–166908
USN Production	4	166911–166914
USN Production	14	166947–166960
USN Production	18	168353–168370
USN Production	4	168463–168466
USN Production	10	168469, 168471–168478, 168483
USN Production	23	168865–168887
USN Production	2	168891–168892
USN Production	8	168920–168927
USN Production	8	169114–169121,169123
TOTAL	**298**	

F/A-18F Two-Seat Super Hornet Program History

Type	Quantity	BuNo
EMD	2	165166, 165170
USN Production	4	166855–166858
USN Production	5	165541–165544
USN Production	12	165668–165679
USN Production	26	165793–165808
USN Production	21	165875–165895
USN Production	19	166449–166467
USN Production	32	166610–166641
USN Production	27	166658–166684
USN Production	36	166790–166816
USN Production	20	166873–166892
USN Production	10	166915–166924
USN Production	4	166961, 166964, 166968, 166969
USN Production	6	166973–166978
RAAF	1	166981
RAAF	24	167957–167980
USN Production	9	168469, 168471–168478
USN Production	9	168485–168493
USN Production	3	168888–168890
USN Production	3	168928–168930
Total	**273**	

A pair of F/A-18F aircraft from VFA-106 are shown on the tarmac at Republic Airport during a visit in May 2019. *Ken Neubeck*

F/A-18F Super Hornets from VFA-106 "Gladiators" are visiting Republic Airport in Long Island, in May 2009, as shown in these two photos. As with the legacy Hornet in US Navy service, the paint scheme is Navy gray. *Ken Neubeck*

F/A-18F Super Hornet from VFA-106 is performing a landing on a conventional runway instead of a carrier deck at Republic Airport in Long Island for an air show appearance. The "Gladiators" have provided two Super Hornets for a demonstration team that appears at air shows throughout the years. *Ken Neubeck*

F/A-18F Super Hornets from VFA-106 are preparing for a dual side-by-side takeoff after completing an air show demonstration during the Jones Beach (New York) Air Show in May 2012. *Ken Neubeck*

The F/A-18 Super Hornet is a very versatile aircraft. During air show performances in which the Super Hornet is not loaded with any ordnance, the pilot is able to perform maneuvers that show the ability of the aircraft. At the New York Air Show in 2015, this Super Hornet from VFA-106 is shown in inverted flight. *Ken Neubeck*

During the New York Air Show in 2015, the aircraft is performing a sharp bank maneuver, which reveals details of the lower fuselage such as the rectangular engine inlet. *Ken Neubeck*

During the New York Air Show in 2015, the F/A-18 Super Hornet is performing a touch-and-go maneuver in which the landing gear is lowered and then pulled up again. *Ken Neubeck*

The Super Hornet performs at high speeds, which create the effect of water vapor lifting off the wings of the aircraft, as seen here. *Ken Neubeck*

F/A-18F Super Hornet from VFA-106 "Gladiators" is on the tarmac of Stewart Airport, New York, prior to its performance at the 2015 New York Air Show. VFA-106 is an active demonstration team that goes to different air shows to demonstrate the aerial capabilities of the Super Hornet. *Ken Neubeck*

This view of an F/A-18F Super Hornet shows all wing pylons loaded with missiles. The arresting gear can be seen stowed in the tail section. *John Gourley*

Another view of the same aircraft during inverted flight shows the profile, with the missiles protruding. *John Gourley*

CHAPTER 2

Super Hornet Features

The left and right main landing gears for the Super Hornet are identical to the legacy Hornets, with the distinctive rear-extending strut assembly. *John Gourley*

The nose landing gear for the Super Hornet is also identical to the legacy Hornets. The main landing-gear actuator is located behind the gear, and there is a catapult launch bar located in front of the landing-gear assembly. *John Gourley*

Forward of the nose landing gear for the Super Hornet is a panel that contains one of the broadband antennas for the aircraft. *John Gourley*

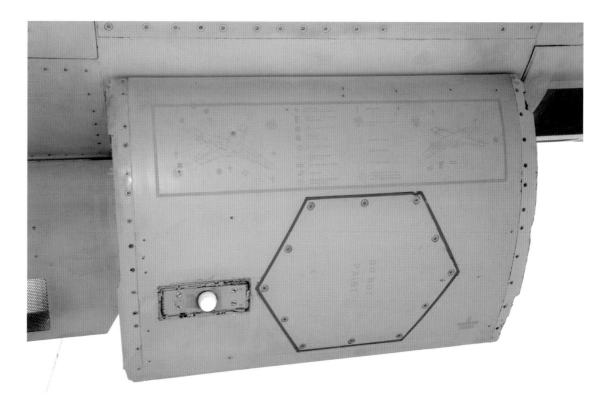

On the inside of the door, the antenna can be accessed by maintenance crew. *John Gourley*

A quick way to distinguish the Super Hornet from the legacy Hornet aircraft is that the Super Hornet has a rectangular inlet structure in lieu of a round intake used by the legacy aircraft.
Ken Neubeck

The larger inlet intake allows for increased airflow to the upgraded F-414-GE-400 engines over the legacy Hornet model.
John Gourley

This is a view of the engine blades that compose the input section of the GE engine, inside the intake. *John Gourley*

Rear view of the exhaust section of the Super Hornet shows the exhaust section of the F-414-GE-400 engine. *John Gourley*

F414-GE-400 engine being tested on maintenance deck of carrier. This engine is more powerful and larger than the F404 engine series used in the legacy Hornets. *US Navy photo by MCS 3rd Class Will Tyndall*

F/A-18E aircraft can be refueled on the deck of the carrier, as seen here with personnel refueling Super Hornet on the deck of the USS *George Washington* in August 2014. *US Navy photo by MCS 3rd Class Chris Cavagnaro*

As with all US fighter aircraft, the Super Hornet has in-flight aerial-refueling capabilities. Here an F/A-18F receives fuel through a receptacle in the nose from a KC-135 fuel tanker. *US Navy photo by MCS 1st Class Trevor Welsh*

Close-up view of an F/A-18E during aerial refueling shows the fuel receptacle probe extending from the right side of the top of the nose to receive fuel from tanker aircraft hose. *US Navy photo by Lt. j.g. Joe Painter*

Not only is the Super Hornet able to be refueled in flight, but it can refuel other US military aircraft from the external fuel pod. In addition to being able to refuel other Super Hornet aircraft, the Super Hornet has refueled EA-6B Prowler aircraft such as this aircraft from VAQ-140, being refueled by an F/A-18E from VFA-143 in October 2012. *US Navy photo by MCS 1st Class Nathanael Miller*

In addition to the ability of being able to conduct in-flight refueling on US military aircraft, the Super Hornet is also capable of performing aerial refueling on foreign military aircraft, such as this French Rafale fighter being refueled by an F/A-18E from VFA-81 in 2015. *US Navy*

Various equipment is packed into the nose of the Super Hornet, including antennas and the 20 mm Gatling gun. *John Gourley*

The M61A2 seven-barrel, 20 mm Gatling gun is seen here outside the F/A-18 Super Hornet aircraft. The barrels are 6 feet in length, and the ammo drum, which holds 412 rounds, is located below the gun. *US Navy photo by MCS Seaman Matthew C. Haws*

The M61A2 20 mm Gatling gun can be removed from the Super Hornet for servicing in the maintenance bay of the carrier. The gun is designed by General Dynamics. *US Navy photo by MCS Seaman Pasquale Sena*

The M61A2 20 mm Gatling gun weighs 202 pounds and with the feed system and full complement of 20 mm shells in the ammo drum weighs 683 pounds. The ammo drum can hold up to 412 rounds and can fire at a maximum rate of 100 rounds per second. *General Dynamics*

Bomb loader crew prepares to load 1,000-pound Mk. 83 bombs onto a BRU-55/A dual-bomb-rack unit mounted on the inboard wing pylon. *US Navy photo by PM 3rd Class Tyler J. Clements*

The use of the BRU-55/A dual-bomb-rack unit on each weapon pylon expands the weapon load capability for each wing pylon of the Super Hornet from one to two. The pilot inspects the installation during preflight inspection. *US Navy photo by PM 3rd Class Tyler J. Clements*

This is one of the early configurations of weapons that are loaded on the Super Hornet. Located on the outboard of the right wing is the AGM-88E High Speed Anti-radiation Missile (HARM). The inboard pylons, where the load can be the heaviest, holds GBU-24 laser-guided bombs. The Joint Direct Attack Munitions (JDAMs) are on the center pylons. *John Gourley*

The same bomb load configuration is on the left wing as well on this aircraft. The gray collar that is fitted around the JDAM munition in the middle of the wing is a kit that provides GPS to make the dumb bomb a precision-guide bomb for accurate drops. *John Gourley*

This is the inboard weapons station, located under the right wing. Standard bomb rack unit for conventional munitions is located toward the front of the pylon, with a missile launcher located farther back on the pylon. The Super Hornet has a lot of flexibility in regard to the different types of ordnance that can be loaded, aiding in its attack mission capability. *John Gourley*

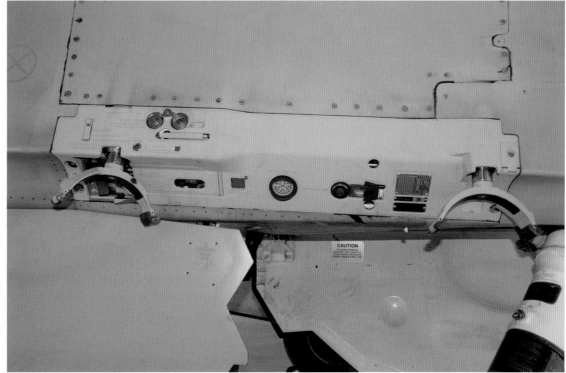

This is another missile launcher unit located on another wing pylon. The two half-circle structures on either end of the unit are sway braces, which provide stability to the missile when in carriage. The electrical connector located in the middle of the unit connects to a cable from the missile for electrical signal interface. *John Gourley*

The Super Hornet has its share of quick-access panels for maintainers to perform various maintenance actions while in one of the bays in the aircraft carrier. Here maintainers from the USS *George H. W. Bush* are lowering the panel for access to the generator. *US Navy photo by MCS 3rd Class Leonard Adams*

Two maintainers from the USS *George H. W. Bush* open the lower fuselage doors of a Super Hornet to perform visual inspection in the aircraft's hydraulic system area. *US Navy photo by MCS 3rd Class Leonard Adams*

Engine maintenance is performed on the carriers. Here, maintainers from the USS *Carl Vinson* are working on the GE F404 engine in the engine repair hangar in February 2012. *US Navy photo by MCS 2nd Class James R. Evans*

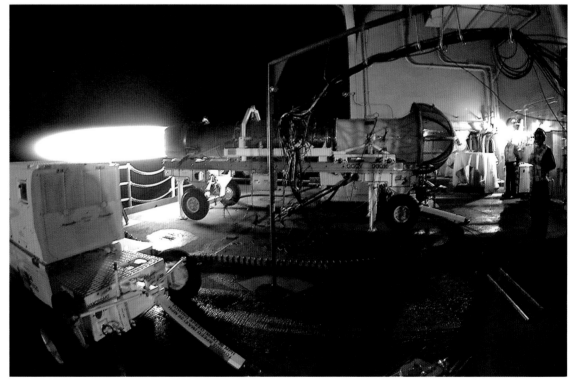

F404 engine is being operated at the edge of the hangar area during checkout by the maintenance crew from the USS *George Washington* in March 2006. Engine maintenance is performed on US carriers. *US Navy photo by MCS 2nd Class Roberto Taylor*

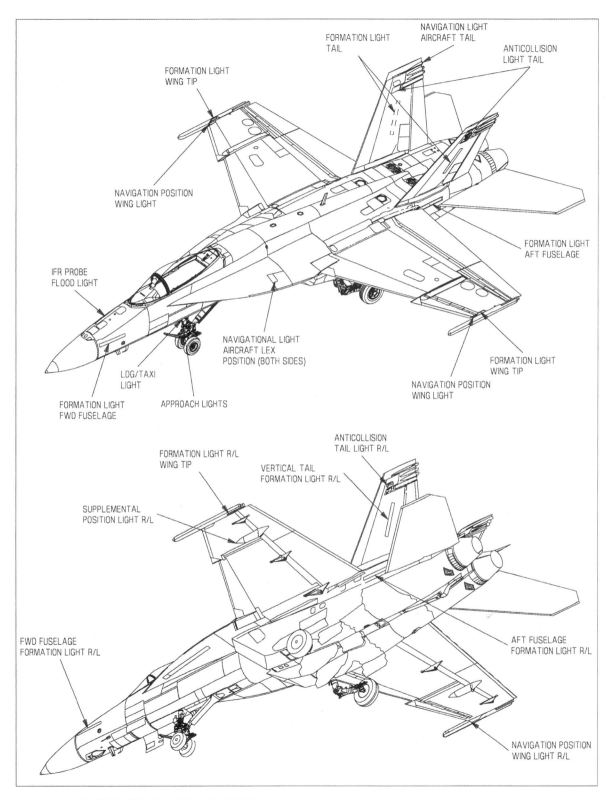

FORMATION LIGHT
TAIL

NAVIGATION LIGHT
AIRCRAFT TAIL

ANTICOLLISION
LIGHT TAIL

FORMATION LIGHT
WING TIP

NAVIGATION POSITION
WING LIGHT

FORMATION LIGHT
AFT FUSELAGE

IFR PROBE
FLOOD LIGHT

NAVIGATIONAL LIGHT
AIRCRAFT LEX
POSITION (BOTH SIDES)

FORMATION LIGHT
WING TIP

NAVIGATION POSITION
WING LIGHT

LDG/TAXI
LIGHT

FORMATION LIGHT
FWD FUSELAGE

APPROACH LIGHTS

FORMATION LIGHT R/L
WING TIP

ANTICOLLISION
TAIL LIGHT R/L

VERTICAL TAIL
FORMATION LIGHT R/L

SUPPLEMENTAL
POSITION LIGHT R/L

FWD FUSELAGE
FORMATION LIGHT R/L

AFT FUSELAGE
FORMATION LIGHT R/L

NAVIGATION POSITION
WING LIGHT R/L

This page from the F/A-18
Super Hornet flight manual
shows all the formation and
navigation light locations on
the aircraft.

There are a number of lights on the Super Hornet. The photo on the left shows the taxi light and the AOA tricolor light panel mounted on the nose landing-gear strut. The above photo shows the set of three taillights on the edge of each vertical stabilizer in the wing section. *John Gourley*

This view from the rear shows the landing-gear setup, along with the some of the access panels opened in the front. *Ken Neubeck*

The trailing edge of the Super Hornet tail flaps is fitted with a boot for dealing with RCS reduction. *John Gourley*

In addition, the trailing edge of the wings is fitted with a boot for RCS reduction. *John Gourley*

There is a conductive coating on all the taillights for Radar Cross Section (RCS) reduction.
John Gourley

Gaps around several of the aircraft's panels are filled in with sealant or tape to reduce RCS.
John Gourley

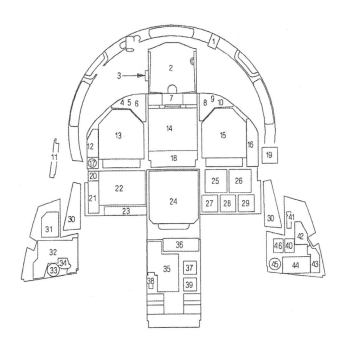

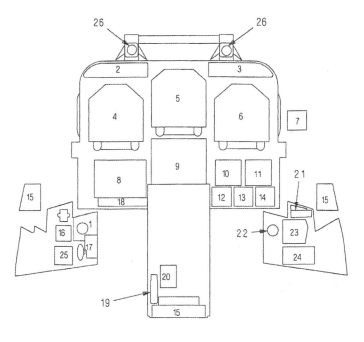

1. LOCK SHOOT LIGHTS
2. HEAD UP DISPLAY (HUD)
3. ANGLE OF ATTACK INDEXER LIGHTS
4. LEFT ENGINE FIRE WARNING/
   EXTINGUISHER LIGHT
5. MASTER CAUTION LIGHT
6. LEFT WARNING/CAUTION/ADVISORY LIGHTS
7. HUD VIDEO CAMERA CONTROL
8. RIGHT WARNING/CAUTION/ADVISORY LIGHTS
9. AUXILIARY POWER UNIT FIRE WARNING/
   EXTINGUISHER LIGHT
10. RIGHT ENGINE FIRE WARNING/EXTINGUISHER
    LIGHT
11. CANOPY INTERNAL JETTISON HANDLE
12. MASTER ARM PANEL
13. LEFT DIGITAL DISPLAY INDICATOR (DDI)
14. UP FRONT CONTROL DISPLAY
15. RIGHT DIGITAL DISPLAY INDICATOR (DDI)
16. SPIN RECOVERY PANEL
17. EMERGENCY JETTISON BUTTON
18. HUD CONTROL
19. STANDBY MAGNETIC COMPASS
20. STATION JETTISON SELECT
21. LANDING GEAR AND FLAP POSITION
    LIGHTS
22. ENGINE FUEL DISPLAY
23. VIDEO RECORD PANEL
24. MULTIPURPOSE COLOR DISPLAY
25. STANDBY ATTITUDE REFERENCE
    INDICATOR

26. BLANK PANEL
27. STANDBY AIRSPEED INDICATOR
28. STANDBY ALTIMETER
29. STANDBY VERTICAL VELOCITY INDICATOR
30. ENVIRONMENT CONTROL LOUVERS
31. LANDING GEAR HANDLE AND WARNING
    TONE SILENCE BUTTON
32. SELECT JETTISON BUTTON
33. BRAKE ACCUMULATOR PRESSURE GAGE
34. EMERGENCY AND PARKING BRAKE HANDLE
35. ECM PANEL
36. BLANK PANEL
37. CLOCK
38. RUDDER PEDAL ADJUST LEVEL
39. COCKPIT ALTIMETER
40. AIRCRAFT BUREAU NUMBER
41. ARRESTING HOOK HANDLE AND LIGHT
42. LANDING CHECKLIST
43. AV COOL SWITCH
44. CAUTION LIGHTS PANEL
45. HYD 1 AND HYD 2 PRESSURE INDICATOR
46. WING FOLD SWITCH

1. EMERGENCY JETTISON BUTTON
2. LEFT WARNING/ADVISORY PANEL
3. RIGHT WARNING/ADVISORY PANEL
4. LEFT DIGITAL DISPLAY INDICATOR (DDI)
5. MULTIPURPOSE COLOR DISPLAY (MPCD)
6. RIGHT DIGITAL DISPLAY INDICATOR (DDI)
7. STANDBY MAGNETIC COMPASS
8. ENGINE FUEL DISPLAY
9. UP FRONT CONTROL DISPLAY
10. STANDBY ATTITUDE REFERENCE INDICATOR
11. BLANK PANEL
12. STANDBY AIRSPEED INDICATOR
13. STANDBY ALTIMETER
14. STANDBY RATE OF CLIMB INDICATOR
15. ENVIRONMENT CONTROL LOUVERS
16. EMERGENCY LANDING GEAR HANDLE AND LIGHT
17. EMERGENCY BRAKE HANDLE AND LIGHT
18. HEADING AND COURSE SET SWITCHES AND
    VIDEO RECORD SWITCHES
19. RUDDER PEDAL ADJUST LEVER
20. AIRCRAFT BUREAU NUMBER
21. SEAT CAUTION MODE SWITCH
22. HYD 1 AND HYD 2 PRESSURE INDICATOR
23. COMMAND SELECTOR VALVE
24. CAUTION LIGHT PANEL
25. COCKPIT ALTIMETER
26. CHAFF/FLARE DISP SWITCHES

General instrument and display arrangement is shown above for the main console of the forward station
for the F/A-18E and F/A-18F, as well as for the rear station for the F/A-18F. Instruments for the rear
stations are not associated with flight control.

Crew from VFA-103 "Jolly Rogers" remove a seat bucket from the Martin Baker ejection seat, sans cushions, in an F/A-18F Super Hornet during maintenance. The ejection rails and brackets remain in the aircraft. *US Navy photo by MCS 3rd Class Jacob Smith*

Maintenance personnel from VFA-195 squadron is working on the ejector components on the Martin Baker ejection seat rails, with seat bucket removed from Super Hornet, while on the flight deck of the USS *George Washington*. *US Navy photo by MCS 3rd Class Bryan Mai*

Maintenance personnel from VFA-27 squadron is working on one of the multifunction displays located in the main console of a Super Hornet, inside the maintenance hangar in the USS *Kitty Hawk*. *US Navy photo by PM 1st Class Hana'lei Shimana*

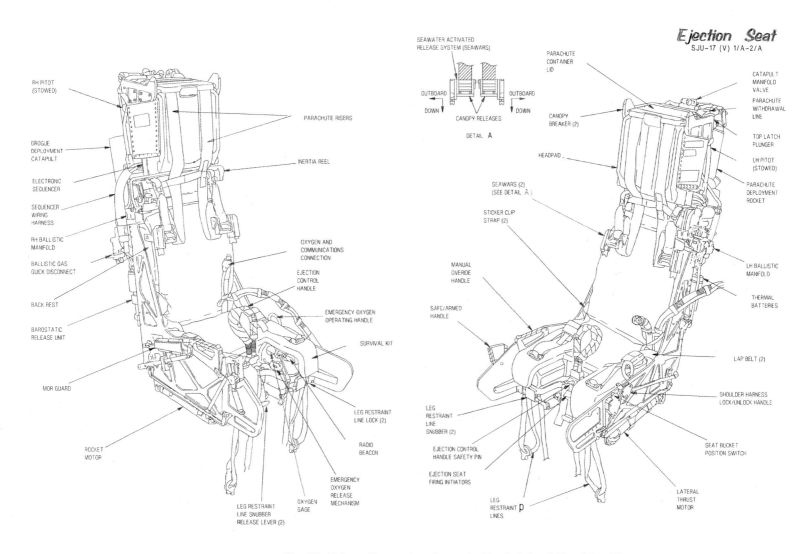

Ejection Seat
SJU-17 (V) 1/A-2/A

RH PITOT (STOWED)

PARACHUTE RISERS

DROGUE DEPLOYMENT CATAPULT

INERTIA REEL

ELECTRONIC SEQUENCER

SEQUENCER WIRING HARNESS

RH BALLISTIC MANIFOLD

OXYGEN AND COMMUNICATIONS CONNECTION

EJECTION CONTROL HANDLE

BALLISTIC GAS QUICK DISCONNECT

EMERGENCY OXYGEN OPERATING HANDLE

BACK REST

SURVIVAL KIT

BAROSTATIC RELEASE UNIT

MOR GUARD

LEG RESTRAINT LINE LOCK (2)

RADIO BEACON

ROCKET MOTOR

EMERGENCY OXYGEN RELEASE MECHANISM

LEG RESTRAINT LINE SNUBBER RELEASE LEVER (2)

OXYGEN GAGE

SEAWATER ACTIVATED RELEASE SYSTEM (SEAWARS)

OUTBOARD

DOWN

OUTBOARD

DOWN

CANOPY RELEASES

DETAIL A

PARACHUTE CONTAINER LID

CANOPY BREAKER (2)

HEADPAD

SEAWARS (2) (SEE DETAIL A)

STICKER CLIP STRAP (2)

MANUAL OVERIDE HANDLE

SAFE/ARMED HANDLE

LEG RESTRAINT LINE SNUBBER (2)

EJECTION CONTROL HANDLE SAFETY PIN

EJECTION SEAT FIRING INITIATORS

LEG RESTRAINT LINES

CATAPULT MANIFOLD VALVE

PARACHUTE WITHDRAWAL LINE

TOP LATCH PLUNGER

LH PITOT (STOWED)

PARACHUTE DEPLOYMENT ROCKET

LH BALLISTIC MANIFOLD

THERMAL BATTERIES

LAP BELT (2)

SHOULDER HARNESS LOCK/UNLOCK HANDLE

SEAT BUCKET POSITION SWITCH

LATERAL THRUST MOTOR

The F/A-18 Super Hornet aircraft uses the Martin Baker SJU-17 (V) or Mk. 14 ejection seat, which is often referred to as Naval Aircrew Ejection Seat (NACES). The basic Mk. 14 seat model has been used on the legacy Hornet and other US Navy aircraft with features as shown above. The seat is propelled out of the aircraft by means of a single three-tube catapult between the main beams and is accelerated by an underseat rocket.

F/A-18 pilot from the VFA-11 "Red Rippers" prepares to leave a Super Hornet aircraft on the USS *Harry S. Truman* in August 2018. *US Navy photo by MCS 2nd Class Thomas Gooley*

F/A-18F pilot and weapons officer from the VFA-211 "Fightin' Checkmates" exit from a Super Hornet aircraft. *US Navy photo by MCS 3rd Class Kaysee Lohmann*

Like all fighter aircraft on aircraft carriers, the F/A-18 Super Hornet is equipped with a tail hook assembly that is used to catch the arresting chain on the carrier deck when the aircraft lands. This photo shows the assembly in the stowed position. *John Gourley*

At the end of the arm is the hook assembly that is used to catch on to the arresting chain. Although rarely used in this case, the arresting hook can be used to grab arresting chains on land-based runways during air shows, as well as if an emergency situation should arise. *John Gourley*

CHAPTER 3
Super Hornet Squadrons

The F/A-18 Super Hornet is currently the mainstay fighter/attack aircraft on US Navy aircraft carriers. Typical configuration for aircraft breakdown per *Nimitz* class aircraft carrier is twenty-four F/A-18C legacy Hornets, twenty-four F/A-E/F Super Hornets, four to five EA-18G Growlers, and a number of other aircraft, including E-2D, C-2, and SH-60.

A brief summary of the fighter/attack aircraft that occupied the US Navy carrier deck from the 1980s up to the present time is presented in the following pages. This is followed by a detailed breakdown of the different Super Hornet squadrons, along with unit insignia.

US Navy Aircraft Carriers and Home Ports		
Ship	**Hull Number**	**Home Port**
Nimitz	CVN-68	Bremerton, Washington
Dwight D. Eisenhower	CVN-69	Norfolk, Virginia
Carl Vinson	CVN-70	San Diego, California
Theodore Roosevelt	CVN-71	San Diego, California
Abraham Lincoln	CVN-72	Norfolk, Virginia
George Washington	CVN-73	Norfolk, Virginia
John C. Stennis	CVN-74	Bremerton, Washington
Harry S. Truman	CVN-75	Norfolk, Virginia
Ronald Reagan	CVN-76	Yokosuka, Japan
George H. W. Bush	CVN-77	Norfolk, Virginia

Active F/A-18E and F Super Hornet Squadrons			
Squadron	**Nickname**	**Tail Code**	**Year to F/A-18E/F**
VFA-2	Bounty Hunters	NE	2003
VFA-11	Red Rippers	AB	2005
VFA-14	Tophatters	NH	2003
VFA-22	Fighting Redcocks	NK	2004
VFA-25	Fist of the Fleet	AG	2013
VFA-27	Royal Maces	NF	2004
VFA-31	Tomcatters	AJ	2006
VFA-32	Swordsman	AC	2004
VFA-34	Blue Blasters	NE	2019
VFA-37	Ragin' Bulls	AC	2019
VFA-41	Black Aces	NH	2001
VFA-81	Sunliners	AA	2008
VFA-83	Rampagers	AC	2018
VFA-86	Sidewinders	AC	2011
VFA-87	Golden Warriors	AJ	2015
VFA-94	Might Shrikes	NA	2016
VFA-97	Warhawks	NG	2013
VFA-102	Diamondbacks	AJ	2004
VFA-103	Jolly Rogers	AG	2004
VFA-105	Gun Slingers	AC	2006
VFA-106	Gladiators	AD	2004
VFA-113	Stingers	AD	2016
VFA-115	Eagles	NF	2002
VFA-122	Flying Eagles	NJ	2010
VFA-131	Wildcats	AC	2019
VFA-136	Knighthawks	AB	2008
VFA-137	Kestrels	NE	2004
VFA-143	Pukin' Dogs	AG	2005
VFA-146	Blue Diamonds	NH	2015
VFA-147	Argonauts	NH	2007
VFA-151	Vigilantes	NC	2013
VFA-154	Black Knights	NH	2007
VFA-192	Golden Dragons	NE	2009
VFA-195	Dambusters	NF	2010
VFA-211	Fighting Checkmates	AB	2010
VFA-213	Blacklions	AJ	2006

During the 1980s, the mix of aircraft that would be on the deck of a typical US aircraft carrier such as the USS *Forrestal*, shown here, consisted of F-14D Tomcats and EA-6B Prowlers, also shown here. *Ray Neubeck*

By 2005, the F-14 Tomcat would be phased out of carrier operation, and F/A-18C Hornets would replace them, while EA-6B continued to serve in the electronic countermeasures (ECM) role, as seen in this photo of these aircraft on the deck of the USS *Harry Truman* during surveillance operations over Iraq in February 2005. *US Navy photo by PH3 Lillian LaVende*

After the beginning of the new millennium, the Super Hornets were being integrated into the US carrier fleet. Two F/A-18E Super Hornets are seen on the right of this photo, joining legacy F/A-18C Hornets on the deck of the *Nimitz* in September 2002, off the California coast. *US Navy photo by Airman Apprentice Mark Rebilas*

This photo shows a collection of F/A-18E Super Hornets on the deck of the *John C. Stennis* in the Pacific Ocean in May 2018. One Super Hornet is preparing for takeoff, with the blast shield on the carrier deck in place. *US Navy photo by MCS 2nd Class David A. Brandenburg*

This photo shows over three dozen aircraft, consisting of F/A-18E Super Hornets and EA-18G Growlers parked on the deck of the *John C. Stennis* in the Pacific Ocean in May 2018. There are three EA-18G Growlers located in the center of the photo, among the Super Hornet aircraft. *US Navy photo by MCS 2nd Class David A. Brandenburg*

F/A-18F (BuNo 165925) from VFA-2 "Bounty Hunters," which has made a stop at Patrick AFB, Florida, in 2003. The aircraft has distinctive markings, such as the light-gray and dark-gray strips on the fuselage and the skull emblem on the tail, along with the NE tail code. The aircraft at that time was assigned to the carrier *Abraham Lincoln*. *John Gourley*

This F/A-18F from VFA-11 "Red Rippers" is flying from the USS *Enterprise* in 2012 and patrolling the Arabian Sea. The US flag is displayed on the side of the cockpit. *US Navy photo by Lt. Cmdr. Josh Hammond*

F/A-18F Super Hornet from VFA-14 "Tophatters" is taking off from the *Nimitz* in 2002. The paint scheme features a distinctive black tail with top-hat emblem in front of the NH tail code. *US Navy photo by PM 3rd Class Yesnia Rosas*

This F/A-18E Super Hornet from VFA-22 "Fighting Redcocks" is landing on the deck of the *Ronald Reagan* during its maiden voyage in January 2006. The Redcock emblem is on the tail, along with the NK tail code. *US Navy photo by PM Airman Gary Prill*

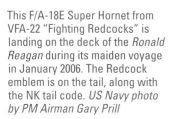

This F/A-18F from VFA-25 "Fist of the Fleet" is flying near the USS *Harry S. Truman* in December 2015, in the Gulf of Oman as part of security operations in the area. This special paint scheme features a fist holding a lightning bolt with yellow and black background. *US Navy photo by Lt. C. Wickware*

F/A-18F from VFA-27 "Royal Maces" is performing touch-and-go maneuvers during carrier air wing qualifications on the USS *Kitty Hawk* near Japan in May 2005. The paint scheme features black upper fuselage and black tail with yellow trim and maces emblem in front of the NF tail code. *US Navy photo by PM 3rd Class Bo Flannigan*

This F/A-18E from VFA-31 "Tomcatters" is taking off from the *George H. W. Bush* in June 2017, in support of Operation Inherent Resolve in the Mediterranean Sea. The tail emblem features a black cat with a bomb, and tail code AJ. *US Navy photo by MCS 2nd Class Christopher Gaines*

This F/A-18F from VFA-32 "Swordsman" is landing on the *Harry S. Truman* in December 2013. The tail artwork features a sword and AC tail code. *US Navy photo by MCS Seaman Blagoj B. Petrovski*

F/A-18C from VFA-34 "Blue Blasters" on the tarmac in Virginia Beach in September 2018. The tail artwork features a skull and sword along with an AE tail code. This squadron has completed its last deployment with F/A-18C Hornets and is to transition to Super Hornets in 2019. *US Navy photo by K. R. Jackson-Smith*

This F/A-18C aircraft from VFA-37 "Ragin' Bulls" is taking off from the *George H. W. Bush* in August 2017. This squadron features a raging-bull emblem and tail code AJ. This squadron also is set to transition to Super Hornet in 2019. *US Navy photo MCS 3rd Class Mario Coto*

This F/A-18F aircraft from VFA-41 "Black Aces" is preparing for launch takeoff from the *Carl Vinson* near the West Coast of the US in February 2002. The paint scheme features an "Ace of Spade" emblem with the NH tail code. *US Navy photo by PM 3rd Class Inez Lawson*

A pair of F/A-18F aircraft from VFA-81 "Sunliners" are secured on the deck of the *Carl Vinson* off Rio de Janeiro in Brazil in February 2010. The paint scheme features a sundial emblem with the AA tail code. *US Navy photo by PM 2nd Class Daniel Barker Lawson*

F/A-18E Super Hornet from VFA-81 is taking off from the USS *Carl Vinson* in the Indian Ocean in May 2015. The aircraft is displayed in special colors for this squadron, including shark's teeth on the forward fuselage. *US Navy photo by MCS 2nd Class John Philip Wagner Jr.*

F/A-18E Super Hornet from VFA-83 "Rampagers" has just landed on the *Dwight D. Eisenhower*, catching the arresting chain on the deck. The aircraft has the AG code on the tails and two different emblems—a ram's-head emblem on the outboard tail section and a charging-bull emblem on the inboard tail section. *US Navy photo by MCS 3RD Class Nathan Parde*

F/A-18E Super Hornet from VFA-86 "Sidewinders" is preparing for a catapult launch from the deck of the *Dwight D. Eisenhower* in December 2015 in the Atlantic Ocean. There is a sidewinder snake emblem in front of the AC tail code on the tail. *US Navy photo by MCS Seaman Anderson W. Branch*

F/A-18E Super Hornet from VFA-87 "Golden Warriors" is preparing for a catapult launch from the deck of the *George H. W. Bush* in November 2016 in the Atlantic Ocean. There is an Indian warrior emblem in front of the AJ tail code on the tail. *US Navy photo by Petty Officer Christopher Gaines*

F/A-18F Super Hornet from VFA-94 "Mighty Shrikes" is taking off from the *Theodore Roosevelt* in February 2018. The aircraft features orange and black trim and the NA tail code. *US Navy photo by MSC 3rd Class Alex Corona*

F/A-18E Super Hornet from VFA-97 "Warhawks" is in flight. The aircraft is from the *John C. Stennis*, based in the Pacific Ocean. The tail features the warhawk emblem with the tail code NG. *US Navy photo by MCS 3rd Class Kenneth Rodriguez*

F/A-18F Super Hornet from VFA-102 "Diamondbacks" is taking off from the USS *Kitty Hawk* in the Pacific Ocean in August 2004. The emblem is diamond shaped, with a diamondback snake. Tail code is NE. *US Navy photo by PH 3rd Class Jason T. Poplin*

This F/A-18F Super Hornet, with special paint scheme, from VFA-102 is taking off from the USS *Kitty Hawk* in the Pacific Ocean in November 2005. The scheme is in recognition of the squadron's fiftieth birthday. The emblem is the head of a diamondback snake, and "50" is painted on the nose. *US Navy photo by PHAN Jonathan Chandler*

F/A-18F Super Hornet from VFA-103 "Jolly Rogers" is in the process of takeoff from the *Abraham Lincoln* in August 2018. The tail features the skull and crossbones, along with some of the squadrons that the aircraft served with on the inside tail. Tail code for VFA-103 is AG. *US Navy photo by MCS Seaman Will Hardy*

F/A-18E Super Hornet from VFA-105 "Gun Slingers" is about to make an arrested landing on the *Theodore Roosevelt* during sea trials in April 2006. The tail code is AC and features a gunslinger emblem. *US Navy photo by PM 3rd Class Chris Thamann*

This F/A-18F aircraft from VFA-106 "Gladiators" is taxiing from Republic Airport during an appearance at an air show demonstration in May 2012. The tail features a Gladiator emblem and AD tail code. *Ken Neubeck*

This F/A-18F aircraft, also from VFA-106, is performing maneuvers during the New York Air Show in August 2015. The emblem is slightly different, with the gladiator figure located inside a shield. *Ken Neubeck*

F/A-18F Super Hornet from VFA-113 "Stingers" is preparing for takeoff from the *Theodore Roosevelt* in the Arabian Gulf in February 2018. The artwork on the tail features a outline drawing of a bee, along with tail code NA. *US Navy photo by MCS 3rd Class Spencer Roberts*

This F/A-18E Super Hornet, BuNo 168877, also from VFA-113, is preparing for arrested landing on the carrier *Theodore Roosevelt* in October 2017 in the Pacific Ocean. There is enhanced artwork on the aircraft, with the bee on the tail being in full color and located inside a shield. *US Navy photo by Lt. Aaron B. Hicks*

This F/A-18E aircraft from VFA-115 "Eagles" has dropped its arresting hook in preparation for landing on the *Ronald Reagan* in June 2016 in the Pacific Ocean. This aircraft features a black paint scheme on the top fuselage, along with eagle emblem on the tail, along with tail code NF. VFA-115 was the first US Navy squadron to use the Super Hornet, beginning in 2002, with support of Operation Enduring Freedom and Operation Southern Watch. *US Navy photo by Lt. Chris Pagenkopf*

This F/A-18E aircraft from VFA-122, the "Flying Eagles," is undergoing preflight inspection by the pilot in March 2005 at NAS Lemoore, California. The tail code is NJ, with the eagle emblem on the leading edge of the tail. *US Navy photo by PM 3rd Class Ronald Gutridge*

This F/A-18E aircraft from VFA-131 "Wildcats" is in flight over NAS Oceana in October 2018. The tail code is AC, with the eagle emblem on the leading edge of the tail. *US Navy photo by MCS 3rd Class Nathan T. Beard*

This F/A-18E aircraft from VFA-136 "Knight Hawks" is on the tarmac of Patrick AFB during a visit in June 2014. The tail code is AB, and the emblem shows a hawk. *John Gourley*

This F/A-18E aircraft from VFA-137 "Kestrels" is taking off from USS *George Washington* in October 2015. The tail code is NE, and the emblem shows a bird. *US Navy photo by MCS 3rd Class Bryan Mai*

F/A-18E aircraft from VFA-143 "Pukin' Dogs" is taking off from USS *Harry S. Truman* during security operations in the Arabian Gulf in February 2016. The tail code is AG, and the emblem is a rabid dog. The extension bar on the nose landing gear is extended during the steam-assisted takeoff. *US Navy photo by MCS Seaman Lindsay A. Preston*

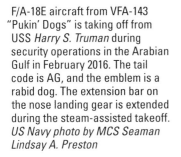

This F/A-18E aircraft from VFA-146 "Blue Diamonds" is taking off from the USS *Nimitz* during training in April 2017 in the Pacific Ocean. The tail code is NH, and the motif is a diamond emblem. *US Navy photo by MCS Seaman Cole Schroeder*

This F/A-18E aircraft from VFA-147 "Argonauts" is launched from the carrier *Nimitz* in May 2014. The aircraft has a special paint scheme, with black on the upper fuselage and red lettering. The tail code is NH, and the emblem consists of a sword and helmet on the tail. *US Navy photo by MCS Seaman Kelly M. Agee*

This F/A-18E aircraft from VFA-151 "Vigilantes" is being launched from the carrier *John C. Stennis* during exercises in the South China Sea in May 2016. The aircraft has tail code markings of NC, and the unit emblem. *US Navy photo by MCS 3rd Class Mike Pernick*

This F/A-18F aircraft from VFA-154 "Black Knights" is being launched from the carrier *Nimitz* in December 2016, with the help of a deck petty officer. The aircraft has tail code markings of NH and two black slash marks. *US Navy photo by Seaman Cole Schroeder*

F/A-18E Super Hornet in special paint scheme from VFA-192 "Golden Dragons" is landing on the carrier *Carl Vinson* in January 2017 in the Pacific Ocean. The paint scheme features the top fuselage in blue with yellow trim. The tail features the gold dragon motif and tail code NE. *US Navy photo by MCS 3rd Class Kurtis A. Hatcher*

F/A-18F Super Hornet from VFA-195 "Dambusters" is participating in joint exercises with Japan during Operation Keen Sword 2013, in late November 2012. The aircraft features the name of the squadron on the fuselage, along with an eagle motif on the tail and tail code NF. *US Navy photo by Lt. Colin Crawford*

An F/A-18F Super Hornet from VFA-211 "Fighting Checkmates," landing on the carrier, is doing maneuvers during the NAS Oceania air show in September 2005. The tail features the checkerboard motif and tail code AB. *US Navy photo by PM 2nd Class Daniel J. McLain*

F/A-18F Super Hornet from VFA-213 "Black Lions" is taking off from the carrier *George H. W. Bush* during patrols over the Arabian Sea in May 2017. The black lion motif and AJ tail code are on the tail. *US Navy photo by MCS 3rd Class Christopher Gaines*

CHAPTER 4
Growler Development

The Grumman EA-6B had been in operational service since 1971 with the US Navy and Marines. The aircraft uses four crew members—one pilot and three electronic-countermeasures officers (ECOs). The aircraft and crew had served in several combat actions, from Desert Storm up to current operations in Iraq and Syria. *Ken Neubeck*

For over three decades, the EA-6B Prowler was the workhorse ECM aircraft assigned to US Navy aircraft carriers. However, by the early part of the new millennium, there was a need by the US Navy to replace the aging EA-6B aircraft that were employed in the electronic-jamming role. Thus came the development of the EA-18G Growler by Boeing and the US Navy.

The first EA-18G flight occurred in August 2006, with production following shortly afterward. The first operational electronic squadron for the Growler was VAQ-129 "Vikings," out of Whidbey Island, Washington, followed by the first deployed squadron, VAQ-131 "Scorpions." Although the EA-6B and the EA-18G look dramatically different from each other, the overall weight and other flight characteristics are similar.

One advantage that the EA-18G has over the EA-6B is speed, with a top speed for the Growler reaching 1,190 mph as compared to the Prowler's top speed of 651 mph—almost twice the speed.

The Growler's flight performance is similar to that of the Super Hornets. This attribute enables the Growler to perform escort jamming as well as the traditional standoff jamming mission, during which Growlers will be able to accompany Super Hornets during all phases of an attack mission.

The Growler has more than 90 percent in common with the standard Super Hornet, sharing the airframe, the radar, and some of the weapon systems. Most of the dedicated ECM equipment is mounted in the space in the forward fuselage that was used to house the internal 20 mm cannon of the Super Hornet, as well as in the wingtips.

The EA-18G is well into production and operational service and has seen action in Libya and Iraq to date. Foreign sales for the aircraft have been completed, with Australia having ordered a dozen aircraft to date.

EA-18G Specifications and outline drawing.

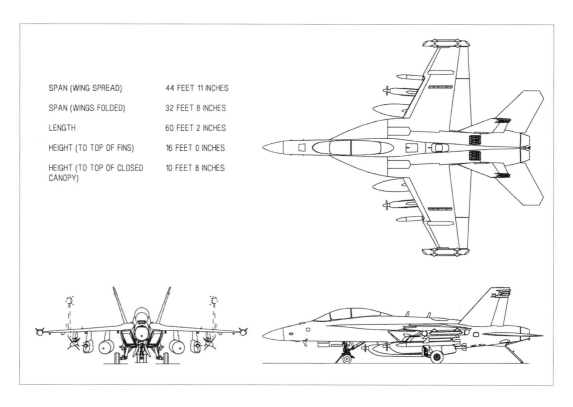

SPAN (WING SPREAD)	44 FEET 11 INCHES
SPAN (WINGS FOLDED)	32 FEET 8 INCHES
LENGTH	60 FEET 2 INCHES
HEIGHT (TO TOP OF FINS)	16 FEET 0 INCHES
HEIGHT (TO TOP OF CLOSED CANOPY)	10 FEET 8 INCHES

Drawing from the EA-18G flight manual shows the location of the EA-18 fuel cells and key equipment.

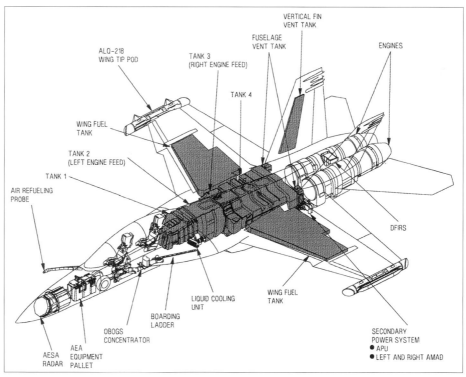

EA-18G & EA-6B Comparison

Characteristics	EA-18G	EA-6B
Weight Empty	33,094 lbs.	33,750 lbs.
Design Gross Wt.	43,900 lbs.	51,000 lbs.
Max Launch Wt.	66,000 lbs.	58,600 lbs.
Available Store Stations	9	5
Internal Fuel	13,940 lbs.	15,422 lbs.
Typical Ext Fuel	6,500 lbs.	4,000 lbs.
Typical Mission Altitude	30,000 ft.	25,000 ft.
Thrust	44,000 lbs.	22,400 lbs.
Spot Factor	1.23	1.26

EA-18G Growler Program History

Type	Quantity	BuNo
Prototype	2	166641–166642
USN Production	4	166855–166858
USN Production	8	166893–166900
USN Production	19	166928–166946
USN Production	25	168250–168274
USN Production	23	168371–168393
USN Production	12	168765–168776
USN Production	12	168931–168942
USN Production	1	168132
RAAF	5	169152–169156
TOTAL	**111**	

This is an EA-18G Growler sans ECM pods. The external appearance of the aircraft resembles the F/A-18F Super Hornet, with the exception of the unique wingtips. *Ken Neubeck*

EA-18G test aircraft (BuNo 1666946) from the US air test and evaluation squadron VX-9 "Vampires" releases decoy flares from the AN/ALE-17 dispenser over the US Navy test range at China Lake, California, in October 2013. *Jamie Hunter*

EA-18G aircraft is undergoing refueling after arriving at Republic Airport in Long Island in June 2010. This aircraft is configured with the full complements of two high-band ECM pods under each wing and one low-band ECM pod under the center fuselage. Additionally, there are two external 480-gallon fuel tanks attached to each inboard wing station. *Ken Neubeck*

Two EA-18Gs are on the tarmac at Republic Airport in October 2011, and both are configured with a single low-band pod under the fuselage and two external fuel tanks under the wings.
Ken Neubeck

EA-18G, BuNo 166896, during landing at Republic Airport in October 2011, shortly after returning to the US after deployment for combat action in Iraq and Libya. *Ken Neubeck*

EA-18G, BuNo 166896, during an early-morning photo at Republic Airport in October 2011. The gold-tinted canopy, which has reflective properties to reduce RF interference to the cockpit, is visible in this photo. *Ken Neubeck*

CHAPTER 5

Growler Features

There is one low-band AN/ALQ-99 pod for this EA-18G, which is mounted under the fuselage. *Ken Neubeck*

There can be up to two high-band AAN/LQ-99 pods for the EA-18G, each mounted on the middle wing station. *Ken Neubeck*

This EA-18G is configured with two wing-mounted high-band ECM pods and one fuselage-mounted low-band ECM pod, along with two external fuel tanks mounted on the inboard pylons. *Ken Neubeck*

The AN/ALQ-99 ECM pods that are used on the EA-18G Growler are the same ECM pods used on the EA-6B Prowler shown here, the aircraft that the EA-18G is replacing. There were 170 EA-6Bs built, and there are over 120 EA-18Gs built to date, including foreign sales. Each pod has a ram air turbine located on the front, with an opening in the rear for air flow exhaust. *Ken Neubeck*

The AN/ALQ-99 ECM pods used on the EA-18G Growler are at the same location on the aircraft as the location used on the EA-6B Prowler—the two outboard wing pylons and the center fuselage. The EA-18G Growler can fly at almost twice the speed as the EA-6B Prowler, at almost 1,200 mph at 40,000 feet. *Ken Neubeck*

An AN/ALQ-99 ECM pod is being loaded to the center of the lower fuselage, behind the nose landing gear of an EA-18G Growler, by loader crew. During transport to the aircraft, the front ram air turbine assembly has a protective cap over it. *US Navy photo by MCS Seaman Apprentice Eleanor D. Vara*

The AN/ALQ-99 ECM pods can be repaired onboard within the electronic repair area, inside the carriers, by an electronic technician, shown here doing some harness repair on a pod. The ALQ-99 system will be used until the next generation of jammer becomes available in 2021. *US Navy photo by MCS 3rd Class David A. Cox*

The EA-18G Growler, like the Super Hornet, has fold-up wings that allow for better parking on the aircraft carrier. Here is a maintenance personnel checking out the outer wing section of a Growler on the USS *Harry S. Truman* in October 2017. *US Navy photo by MCS 3rd Class Tommy Gooley*

The EA-18G is still able to taxi with the outer wing section in the upward position, as seen on this Growler taxiing down the runway of the naval air facility in Misawa, Japan, in January 2013. *US Navy photo by MCS 1st Class Alfredo Rosado*

Located at midnose of the F/A-18E Super Hornet is the muzzle plate for the 20 mm Gatling gun, which has an ammo drum consisting of 412 rounds. *John Gourley*

For the EA-18G Growler, the gun and gun muzzle plate have been removed from the nose, and in their place is ECM equipment such as the ALQ-218 (V) and CCS Receiver and Electronic Attack. *Ken Neubeck*

Additional antennas that were added to the rear spine of the EA-18G include the CCS antenna (*seen on the left*) and the satellite communications antenna (which is the raised bump on the top fuselage). *Ken Neubeck*

Another distinctive characteristic pertaining to the EA-18G as compared to the Super Hornet is that the wingtips now have the AN/ALQ-218 pods attached to them. The antennas are used for the ECM jamming system. *Ken Neubeck*

The EA-18G design is based on the two-seat F/A-18F aircraft, with the front cockpit station dedicated to the pilot, and the rear cockpit station now dedicated to the ECM officer (instead of the weapons systems officer [WSO] from the F/A-18F), who handles the ECM tasks for the aircraft. The EA-18G uses one ECO, in lieu of three ECOs used in the EA-6B. *Ken Neubeck*

This EA-18G from VAQ-132 "Scorpions" has just landed at Republic Airport in October 2011, and the pilot and ECO are in the process of exiting the aircraft. *Ken Neubeck*

When crew members exit the EA-18G Growler, they walk on the black mat area on top of the wing and then extend to the boarding ladder, which is seen here being set up by maintenance personnel.
Ken Neubeck

The ECO is exiting EA-18G Growler from VAQ-132, shortly after arrival at Republic Airport, Long Island, in 2011. The ECO is standing on the black rubber mat prior to walking onto the boarding ladder.
Ken Neubeck

Similar to the F/A-18F Super Hornet, the EA-18G Growler has two ejection seats for the crew, the Martin Baker Mk. 14 (also known as the SJU17A and NACES). *Ken Neubeck*

This is a close-up view of the headrest portion of the Martin Baker Mk. 14, used in the EA-18G Growler. Located behind the forward station ejection seat is the control console for the rear ECO crew member. *Ken Neubeck*

This is the front cockpit station of the EA-18G. It is almost identical to the F/A-18E pilot station. There are three multifunction displays (MFD) located in the top portion of the console (one on the right, one on the left, and one in the center, behind the control stick). The center MFD can be used for displaying terrain images. The Up-Front Control Display (UFCD) is located in the top portion of the console, with the Heads-up Display (HUD) located on the top of the console. The ejection seat can be seen, with the ejection control handle in the front marked in yellow and black. *Jamie Hunter*

This is the rear cockpit station of the EA-18G. In contrast to the rear station of the F/A-18F Super Hornet, the functions are directed toward ECM work by the ECO, in lieu of weapon release functions. As in the F/A-18F, there is no control stick, and there are limited flight control indicators. There are three MFDs, with two located in the top portion of the console (one on the right, one on the left) and a large one in the center of the console. The center MFD is larger in the rear station than the front station and is used for ECM-related tasks. In lieu of the HUD, the UFCD is located on the top of the console. *Jamie Hunter*

The nose landing gear is the same for the Growler as it is for the Super Hornet. A feature that is important for carrier operation is the white box located near the top of the nose landing-gear strut, by the taxi light. This box contains three approach lights of red, amber, and green. The light serves as a visual indicator to the landing-signal officer (LSO) on the carrier for angle-of-attack (AOA) speed, where red is fast, on-speed is amber, and green is slow, as well as indicating that all landing gear are down and locked. When the approach lights flash, it is an indication to the LSO that the arresting hook is not down, and the pilot must be alerted. The nose landing gear has a bar located in front that is used for steam-assisted takeoff from the carrier. *Ken Neubeck*

EA-18G Growler, BuNo 166895, from VAQ-132, is taxiing down the runway in preparation for takeoff from Republic Airport in Long Island in November 2011.
Ken Neubeck

EA-18G Growler, BuNo 166895, is followed by a second EA-18G, BuNo 166896, as they taxi down the runway in preparation for takeoff. Both aircraft are equipped with two 480-gallon external fuel tanks mounted under each wing, for the long trip cross-country back to the home of VAQ-132 in Whidbey Island, Washington.
Ken Neubeck

CHAPTER 6
Growler Squadrons

US Navy EA-18G Growler squadrons use the VAQ designation, which refers to electronic attack squadrons. The earliest electronic squadrons that were activated for the EA-18G Growler were VAQ-129 "Vikings" and VAQ-132 "Scorpions" in 2009. Since then, the list of electronic squadrons using Growlers has grown to fourteen.

Growlers are assigned to the same aircraft carrier as the Super Hornets are assigned. The number of Growler aircraft per carrier can range from four to six.

The following pages show the EA-18G with the different electronic squadrons, along with the unit's insignia.

EA-18G Growler Squadrons			
Squadron	**Nickname**	**Tail Code**	**Year to EA-18G**
VAQ-129	Vikings	NJ	2009
VAQ-130	Zappers	NJ	2011
VAQ-131	Lancers	NJ	2014
VAQ-132	Scorpions	NL	2009
VAQ-133	Wizards	NJ	2014
VAQ-134	Garudas	NJ	2015
VAQ-135	Black Ravens	NJ	2011
VAQ-136	Gauntlets	NE	2013
VAQ-137	Rooks	AB	2013
VAQ-138	Yellow Jackets	NL	2010
VAQ-139	Cougars	NH	2011
VAQ-140	Patriots	AG	2014
VAQ-141	Shadowhawks	NF	2010
VAQ-142	Gray Wolves	NH	2015

This EA-18G from VAQ-139 "Cougars" visited Republic Airport on Long Island, New York, in June 2014. *Ken Neubeck*

EA-18G from VAQ-129 "Vikings" is seen here in a special three-tone blue paint scheme here at Republic Airport in Long Island, New York, during an air show appearance. The Growler is painted in this 1944 retro paint scheme to honor Air Group 85, which operated from the USS *Shangri-La* (CV 34) during World War II. *Ken Neubeck*

The special blue EA-18G is next to a more conventional VAQ-129 Squadron EA-18G at Republic Airport in May 2011. *Ken Neubeck*

The special three-tone paint scheme of VAQ-129 "Vikings" EA-18G (*seen on the opposite page*) is seen here on takeoff. This paint scheme was used in 2011. *US Navy photo by MCS 2nd Class Briana C. Brotzman*

This is the standard paint scheme used by the Vikings' EA-18G, seen here on takeoff. The Vikings are one of the fleet's oldest electronic squadrons in service, having started in 1961 with Douglas A-3 Skywarrior aircraft. *US Navy photo by MCS 3rd Class Rialyn Rodrigo*

EA-18G from VAQ-130 "Zappers" is flying over the Arabian Sea in August 2010 during security operations. The tail artwork consists of a golden lion with a sword and AC tail code. The "Zappers" are another older electronic squadron that started in 1959 with Douglas AD-5Q aircraft. *US Navy photo by MCS 2nd Class Kilho Park*

EA-18G from VAQ-131 "Lancers" is preparing for takeoff from Whidbey Island, Washington, in August 2017. The tail artwork consists of lances and helmet along with the AJ tail code. *US Navy photo by MCS 2nd Class Scott Wood*

EA-18G from VAQ-132 "Scorpions" is preparing for takeoff after an overnight stop at Republic Airport in Long Island in November 2011. *Ken Neubeck*

A close-up view of the VAQ-132 EA-18G shows the tail of the scorpion painted in gray on the tail, followed by the NL tail code, indicating that it is based out of Whidbey Island in Washington. This squadron has been active since 1968 and recently flew EA-6B Prowlers prior to transitioning to EA-18G Growlers. *Ken Neubeck*

EA-18G from VAQ-133 "Wizards" is taking off from the USS *John C. Stennis* in the Pacific Ocean in March 2016. The tail artwork features a lightning bolt with tail code NG. The Wizards squadron began service in 1966. *US Navy photo by MCS 3rd Class Andre R. Richard*

EA-18G from VAQ-134 "Garudas" is preparing for takeoff from base in Anchorage, Alaska, in May 2017. The tail artwork features the mythical Garudas bird with tail code NL. This squadron began service in 1966. *US Navy photo by MCS 3rd Class Travis Litke*

EA-18G from VAQ-135 "Black Ravens" is flying over Oak Harbor, Washington, in 2013. The artwork features a black raven and NL tail code on the tail. This electronic squadron started in 1969 with EKA-3B Skywarriors, which would be replaced with EA-6B Prowlers. *US Navy*

Four EA-18Gs from VAQ-136 "Gauntlets" (established in 1973) are taking off from the USS *Carl Vinson* in April 2017 in the South China Sea. The artwork features a hand holding a sword, with the NE tail code. *US Navy photo by Lt. Andrew DeGarmo*

EA-18G from VAQ-137 "Rooks" is landing on the USS *Theodore Roosevelt* in January 2015 in the Atlantic Ocean. The artwork features a mythical bird and tail code AB on the tail. The squadron started with EA-6B Prowlers in 1973, which are being relieved by the EA-18G Growlers. *US Navy photo by MCS Seaman Apprentice Alex Millar*

This EA-18G from VAQ-138 "Yellow Jackets" (established in 1976) is in flight in December 2011 near Greece. The aircraft was part of a six-month deployment in Iraq as part of Operation New Dawn. The artwork features a yellow jacket and tail code NL on the tail. *US Navy photo by Paul Farley*

EA-18G from VAQ-139 "Cougars" is visiting Republic Airport in Long Island in June 2014. The aircraft does not have any ECM pods attached to its pylons. The unit's emblem, a cougar's head, is painted on the tail and on the external fuel tank on the centerline. *Ken Neubeck*

Closer view of the VAQ-139 aircraft's tail shows the cougar's-head emblem and the NA tail code. Electronic Squadron VAQ-139 began service in July 1983 with EA-6B Prowlers, which was relieved by the EA-18G Growlers. *Ken Neubeck*

EA-18G from VAQ-140 "Patriots" preparing to land with tail hook deployed on the USS *Abraham Lincoln* in the Atlantic Ocean in August 2018. The unit has tail code AG. *US Navy photo by Lt. j.g. Christopher Czapski*

EA-18G, also from VAQ-140 "Patriots," is taking off from the USS *Harry S. Truman* in the Mediterranean Sea during Operation Inherent Resolve in June 2014. This particular aircraft features a special American flag emblem on the tail. *US Navy photo by MCS 3rd class Bobby J. Siens*

EA-18G from VAQ-141 "Shadowhawks" is preparing for takeoff from the USS *George Washington* near Okinawa, Japan, in July 2014. This aircraft has the hawk's-head emblem and NF tail code, along with black trim on the upper fuselage. *US Navy photo by MCS 3rd Class Chris Cavagnaro*

EA-18G from VAQ-142 "Gray Wolves" is in flight over the USS *Nimitz* in October 2016. This aircraft has the gray-wolf emblem and NH tail code. *US Navy photo by Seaman David Claypool*

CHAPTER 7
The Super Hornet and Growler at War

EA-18Gs from VAQ-139 "Cougars" are in flight over Long Island in November 2011, months after their deployment in Libya. *Ken Neubeck*

The legacy F/A-18 Hornet had served in Operation Desert Storm in 1991 and in Kosovo in 1998. With the Super Hornet achieving initial operating capability (IOC) in 2001, the first combat action that the aircraft would see was during Operation Southern Watch, in which an F/A-18E dropped JDAM bombs in Iraq in November 2002. Subsequently, during Operation Iraqi Freedom, beginning in 2003, Super Hornets from VFA-14, VFA-41, and VFA-115 flew a multitude of missions, including close air support, strike, escort, and aerial refueling, with the latter mission being performed by aircraft from VFA-14.

F/A-18 Super Hornets would see action in Afghanistan in September 2006, when F/A-18F aircraft dropped GRU-12 and GRU-38 bombs against Taliban fortifications west and northwest of Kandahar.

F/A-18 Super Hornets would continue to support Operation Iraqi Freedom and Operation Enduring Freedom from 2006 through 2007, with aircraft from VFA-103 and VFA-143 flying from the carrier *Dwight D. Eisenhower* off the coast of Somalia.

In recent years, much of the F/A-18 Super Hornet combat action has been focused in the Middle East, more specifically against the forces of ISIS located in Iraq and Syria. The Super Hornets are launched from carriers situated in the Arabian Sea. In addition to the bombing of strategic targets against ISIS, the Super Hornet has engaged enemy aircraft in these areas.

On June 18, 2017, Lt. Cmdr. Michael Tremel, in an F/A-18E Super Hornet from VFA-87 that was launched from the carrier USS *George H. W. Bush*, shot down a Sukhoi Su-22 Syrian fighter jet south of Tabqah after it had dropped bombs near the US-backed Syrian Democratic Forces. His first shot was with an AIM-9X Sidewinder missile, but the Su-22 deployed decoy flares, which caused the missile to miss. A second radar-guided AIM-120 AMRAAM missile was then fired, which destroyed the Su-22. The Su-22 pilot bailed out over ISIS-controlled territory. It was the first time a US pilot made an air-to-air kill since the Kosovo conflict in 1999.

The EA-18G Growler completed IOC in 2011, and five Growlers from VAQ-132 "Scorpions" were sent to Libya to jam enemy radar during Operation Odyssey Dawn, beginning in March 2011.

Since 2014, the EA-18G has been deployed into the Arabian Gulf in support of operations against ISIS in the region of northern Iraq and Syria. Participating squadrons have included the VAQ-139 "Cougars" and VAQ-137 "Rooks."

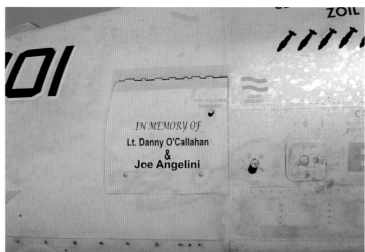

Photos above show different F/A-18 Super Hornet artwork on the inboard pylons, honoring victims of the September 11, 2001, attacks in New York City. The aircraft are assigned to the *Abraham Lincoln*, which was deployed to the Arabian Gulf in 2002 in support of Operation Iraqi Freedom, which began in 2003. *US Navy photo by PH3 Michael S. Kelly*

Two FA-18E Super Hornets from VFA-31 are flying over Afghanistan in December 2009 during patrols there. *USAF photo by SSgt. Aaron Allmon*

Four FA-18F Super Hornets are flying over the mountains of Afghanistan in November 2010, in support of operations there. *USAF photo by SSgt. Andy M. Kin*

F/A-18F Super Hornet from VAQ-41 "Black Aces" is flying over Afghanistan in October 2009, in support of US operations conducted there. *US Navy photo by Lt. j.g. Kyle Terwillger*

F/A-18F Super Hornet from VAQ-41 is in the process of refueling during a mission over Afghanistan in December 2009. Photos of F/A-18 Super Hornets in Afghanistan are often taken by USAF personnel working from the USAF tankers. *USAF photo by SSgt. Michael B. Keller*

Five EA-18G Growlers from VAQ-132 "Scorpions" participated in jamming enemy radar during Operation Odyssey Dawn in Libya, beginning in March 2011. This was the first combat action for the Growlers. Here are the Growlers as they do a flyby over their home base in Whidbey Island, Washington, in July 2011.
US Navy photo by MCS 2nd Class Nardel Gervacior

Here is a close-up of one of the EA-18G Growlers from VAQ-132 during a stop at Republic Airport in Long Island, New York, in November 2011, not long after Operation Odyssey Dawn. This visit was part of a promotional visit to nearby Northrop Grumman.
Ken Neubeck

Two EA-18G Growlers from VAQ-139 "Cougars" are in flight in the Arabian Sea during operations against ISIS in Iraq and Syria in November 2014. Both aircraft are equipped with the full complement of jamming pods—two high band and one low band, along with two external fuel tanks. *US Navy photo by MCS 2nd Class John Philip Wagner Jr.*

EA-18G Growler from VAQ-139 is taking off from the deck of the USS *Carl Vinson* in December 2014 in the Arabian Sea, during operations against ISIS in the region. *US Navy photo by MCS 2nd Class John Philip Wagner Jr.*

With US aircraft carrier in the waters in the region near Iraq and Syria, the F/A-18 Super Hornet was very active in attacks on ISIS targets in 2017, such as this fully loaded Super Hornet aircraft with ten Mk. 82 500-pound bombs loaded under the wing, ready to go on a bombing mission. *US Navy photo by MCS 2nd Class Hank Gettys*

Close-up view of the left wing of the Super Hornet shows a pair of the BRU-55 dual bomb carriers along with the outboard wing pylon holding a single bomb. The BRU-55 expands the weapon load capability for the F/A-18 Super Hornet. *US Navy photo by MCS 3rd Class Matt Matlage*

This F/A-18E Super Hornet from VFA-81 "Sunliners" is taking off with conventional munitions ordnance with JDAM guidance under each wing, from the USS *Carl Vinson* in February 2015. *US Navy photo by MCS 2nd Class John Philip Wagner Jr.*

This F/A-18E Super Hornet from VFA-136 "Knight Hawks" is taking off with a full load of ordnance under each wing, using the dual bomb rack BRU-55, from the USS *Theodore Roosevelt* in May 2015. The type of mission flown dictates the weapon load used. *US Navy photo by MCS 3rd Class Anna Van Nuys*

This RAAF F/A-18F Super Hornet BuNo 167972, is photographed in Hawaii after landing. This aircraft is assigned to RAAF No. 6 Squadron out of Amberly, Australia. *USAF photo by TSgt. Michael R. Holzworth*

As of 2019, the only foreign sales of the Super Hornet aircraft as well as Growler aircraft have been to the Royal Australian Air Force (RAAF). In May 2007, the Australian government signed a contract for twenty-four F/A-18F Super Hornets. These are to replace the F-111 Aardvarks that were in Australian service.

The contract was temporarily modified in February 2009 to change twelve of the twenty-four Super Hornets on order to be replaced on the production line as EA-18G Growlers. Eventually this would change; the original order of twenty-four F/A-18G would remain intact, and the RAAF would receive an additional twelve EA-18G Growlers.

The RAAF has been operating the Super Hornet since 2010 and has supported operations in the war against ISIS in the Middle East, in conjunction with the United States. There are two RAAF squadrons operating the Super Hornet: No. 1 and No. 6 Squadrons, with twelve aircraft each.

Canada considered buying the Super Hornet in lieu of the F-35 to replace their CF-18 aircraft in service. However, the current option on the table is for Canada to buy Australian F/A-18 Hornets as a potential replacement.

In July 2018, it was announced by Boeing that a deal was in place for Kuwait to purchase twenty-eight Super Hornets. The proposed mix would be twenty-two single-seat (E model) and six two-seat (F model) Super Hornets to be delivered by 2022. There is also an option for an additional twelve Super Hornets, for a total order of forty aircraft.

The Super Hornet is also being considered as an option by several countries in Europe, as well as by India in lieu of using the F-35.

An overview of RAAF F/A-18F aircraft being refueled during Operation Inherent Resolve over the Middle East, during war efforts against ISIS in March 2016. This Super Hornet features a kangaroo emblem on the fuselage, along with squadron marking and Australian flag on the tail. The aircraft has bombing-mission markings on the forward fuselage. *USAF photo by TSgt. Nathan Lipsomb*

An overview of RAAF F/A-18F aircraft being refueled during Operation Inherent Resolve over the Middle East, during war efforts against ISIS in July 2017. This Super Hornet was originally BuNo 167959, then was changed to RAAF number A44-203, and is one of several RAAF aircraft working with the US in the war against ISIS. *USAF photo by TSgt. Amy Lovgren*

A close-up view of RAAF F/A-18F aircraft being refueled during Operation Inherent Resolve in the war on ISIS in July 2017. The Australian flag can be seen draped over the top of the rear console. *USAF photo by TSgt. Amy Lovgren*

CHAPTER 9

The Future

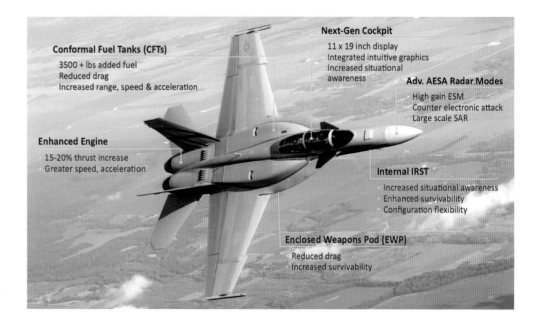

Conformal Fuel Tanks (CFTs)
3500 + lbs added fuel
Reduced drag
Increased range, speed & acceleration

Next-Gen Cockpit
11 x 19 inch display
Integrated intuitive graphics
Increased situational awareness

Adv. AESA Radar Modes
High gain ESM
Counter electronic attack
Large scale SAR

Enhanced Engine
15-20% thrust increase
Greater speed, acceleration

Internal IRST
Increased situational awareness
Enhanced survivability
Configuration flexibility

Enclosed Weapons Pod (EWP)
Reduced drag
Increased survivability

Features shown above are the proposed additions to the Super Hornet Block III aircraft. *Boeing*

The F/A-18 Super Hornet has an excellent future for the coming years. Beside the possibility of additional sales to foreign countries, recent upgrades of the aircraft will allow it to stay in US Navy service.

Boeing and the US Navy are upgrading the Super Hornet to a new Block III standard, under which 116 new Super Hornets will be built. In addition, approximately 540 existing Super Hornets will be upgraded to Block II standard.

The Block II upgrades consisted of the incorporation of an improved APG-76 active electronically scanned array (AESA) radar, as well as larger displays, along with the joint helmet-mounted cuing system and several other avionics replacements. The Block III standard consists of the following changes:

Conformal fuel tanks (CFTs)
Infrared search and track capability
Coatings to reduce radar signature of aircraft
New mission computers
Single wide-area multifunction display
New lifespan of 9,000 flight hours

The CFTs are a major change in that in lieu of the current configuration of the Super Hornet, carrying two 300-gallon drop tanks under the pylon, the aircraft will have increased fuel capability added inside the fuselage of the aircraft. There is increased aerodynamic efficiency by not having the external tanks, as well as by freeing up two pylons for more ordnance. Flight testing is planned for the CFT to show that there is not significant loss of maneuverability with this added feature.

The current plan for the Block III upgrade is that Boeing will deliver two test jets to the US Navy in 2019. Production will begin in late 2020, and the CFT for these aircraft will finish testing and enter service. In 2022, Boeing will convert existing Block II Super Hornets to Block III Super Hornets, with the first operational Block III squadron deployed in this year.

It is planned that a mix of the Block III Super Hornets complemented with F-35C aircraft will be the configuration of fighter/attack aircraft on the carriers for the future. There is no retirement date planned for the Block III Super Hornet.

First flight of the F/A-18E/F Advanced Super Hornet, with conformal fuel tanks and Enclosed Weapons Pod (EWP), was conducted on August 7, 2013, at the Boeing facility in St. Louis, Missouri. These two features are part of the Block III upgrade. Later flights would be conducted at the US Navy test facility in Pax River, Maryland. *Boeing*

The upgraded cockpit on the Super Hornets Block III will include increased computing power, supporting enhanced graphical data displays, and an 11-by-19-inch touchscreen. *Boeing*

It has been officially announced by the US Navy that the famed Blue Angels team will be transitioning from the F/A-18C and D Hornet aircraft to the F/A-18E and F Super Hornet by the end of 2021. This is a photo of the F/A-18D two-seater during a visit to Republic Airport in Long Island, prior to an air show, in November 2011. *Ken Neubeck*

The Blue Angels team will have to train extensively with the Super Hornet during the winter off-season, beginning in early 2022, at El Centro, California, since it has increased speed and performance characteristics over the existing F/A-18C and D models, which the team has been flying for over thirty years. *Ken Neubeck*

F/A-18F Super Hornet, BuNo 166885, is one of the Top Gun aircraft at the Naval Aviation Warfighting Development Center near Reno, Nevada. The Super Hornet is one of a number of aircraft with skilled trainer pilots used to provide top-level combat skills to US Navy pilots during training courses. *Jamie Hunter*

F/A-18F Super Hornet from VFA-31 is flying with a French navy marine Rafale aircraft during an airshow over Chesapeake Bay, Maryland, in May 2018. *Petty Officer 2nd Class David Mora Jr.*

A pair of F-35C Lighting II aircraft from the Grim Reaper squadron are flying with two Super Hornet aircraft over Fallon, Nevada, in September 2015. A future plan under consideration is that the Department of Defense (DOD) is considering buying more F-35C aircraft, which are carrier based, to replace over 500 Super Hornets. However, currently, the DOD plans to replace the older F/A-18C/D Hornets with 220 Lightning II aircraft. The different plans may not necessarily mean the end of Super Hornet use by the US Navy, but a probable mix of different aircraft models will be used in the immediate future on US Navy carriers. *US Navy photo by MCS 1st Class Joseph R. Vincent*

This F/A-18F Super Hornet from VFA-102 "Diamondbacks" is getting a freshwater wash-down at night on the USS *Ronald Reagan* during deployment in the Philippine Sea in September 2016. The saltwater deposits that accumulate on the airframe when the plane is out at sea have to be washed off regularly in order to avoid corrosion to the metal parts of the aircraft. *US Navy photo by MCS Specialist Jamaal N. Liddell*